I AM FOR
A KOOL-ART,
7-UP ART,
PEPSI-ART,
SUNSHINE ART,
39 CENTS ART ...

CLAES OLDENBURG, 1961

Published by
Art Gallery of New South Wales
Art Gallery Road, The Domain
Sydney 2000, Australia
artgallery.nsw.gov.au

with the exhibition
Pop to popism
Art Gallery of New South Wales
1 November 2014 – 1 March 2015

Art Gallery of New South Wales
Cataloguing-in-publication
Pop to popism / edited by Wayne Tunnicliffe
and Anneke Jaspers
ISBN 9781741741100 (hc)
ISBN 9781741741094 (pb)
1. Pop art – Exhibitions.
2. Pop art – Great Britain – Exhibitions.
3. Pop art – United States – Exhibitions.
4. Pop art – Australia – Exhibitions.
5. Pop art – Europe – Exhibitions.
I. Tunnicliffe, Wayne II. Jaspers, Anneke.
III. Art Gallery of New South Wales.
Includes bibliographic references and index.

ISBN 9783791381329 (hc US edition)

front cover: Roy Lichtenstein *In the car* 1963
(detail), pp 86–87
back cover: Maria Kozic *MASTERPIECES
(Warhol)* 1986, p 279

details:
p 2: Eduardo Paolozzi *I was a rich man's
plaything* 1947, p 22
p 4: Bridgid McLean *Untitled* 1969, p 184
p 8: Richard Hamilton *My Marilyn* 1965, p 53
pp 14–15: Alain Jacquet *Déjeuner sur l'herbe
(diptych)* 1964, p 119

The Art Gallery of New South Wales is a
statutory body of the NSW State Government

Distribution

Australian and New Zealand
Thames & Hudson Australia
11 Central Boulevard, Portside Business
Park, Fishermans Bend, Melbourne 3207
tel: +61 3 9646 7788
email: enquiries@thaust.com.au

North America
Prestel Publishing, a member of the
Verlagsgruppe Random House GmbH
900 Broadway, Suite 603, New York,
NY 10003
tel: +1 212 995 2720
fax: +1 212 995 2733
email: sales@prestel-usa.com
www.prestel.com
ISBN 9783791381329

All other territories
Thames & Hudson UK
181A High Holborn, London WC1V7QX
tel: +44 20 7845 5000
email: sales@thameshudson.co.uk
www.thameshudson.co.uk

Managing editor: Julie Donaldson
Text editor: Paige Amor
Proofreader: Amber Cameron
Rights & permissions: Megan Young,
Isabelle Rouvillois, Jude Fowler Smith
Index: Sherrey Quinn, Libraries Alive

Design: Analiese Cairis
Production: Cara Hickman
Colour reproduction: Spitting Image
Printing and binding: Australian Book
Connection, China

SYDNEYINTERNATIONALARTSERIES

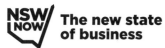 The new state of business

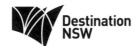 Destination NSW

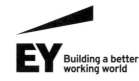 EY Building a better working world

Strategic partners

Principal partner

 TERRA FOUNDATION FOR AMERICAN ART

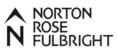 NORTON ROSE FULBRIGHT

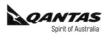 QANTAS Spirit of Australia

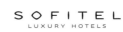 SOFITEL LUXURY HOTELS

Major partners

Official airline

Official hotel partner

 AVANTCard

CREATIVE CITY SYDNEY
CITY OF SYDNEY

 JCDecaux

 PORTER'S ORIGINAL PAINTS

Sydney Airport

The Sydney Morning Herald

Supporting partners

326

politically engaged art 114, 128, 132, 161, 188–91, 196, 222, 230, 294, 298
Polke, Sigmar 112, 113, 114, 297
  Untitled (Vase II) 114, **122**, 303
  Weekend-home **126**, 302
pop art
  beginnings/origins 11–12, 18–21, 60, 188
  characteristics 11, 60, 63, 64–65, 139, 189
  end date 12, 13, 64, 190
  legacy 13, 237
  name/alternate names 11, 21, 37, 62, 112, 188, 190, 281n5(3)
  post-1968 188–231; works **192–231**
  'sinister Pop' 191
  techniques *see* techniques and materials
  see also American pop art; Australian pop art; British pop art; European pop art; popism; post-pop
Pop art 1955–1970 touring exhibition, 1985 237
Pop art USA exhibition, Oakland Art Museum, 1963 76
'Pop goes the easel' (magazine article) 139, 143, 150
Pop goes the easel (TV documentary) 39, 42, 284n7, 293
popism 13, 234–36
Popism exhibition, National Gallery of Victoria, Melbourne, 1982 13, 147, 234, 236, 237, 240, 250
popular culture 11–13, 18–21, 36–39, 42, 60–62, 138, 143, 147, 237 *see also* mass media
popular music 62, 138, 190
post-pop 234–79
  works **238–79**
posters 166–69
postmodernism 12–13, 65, 234, 236, 237, 282n37
Powditch, Peter 145–46, 180, 216, 297, *314*
  Seascape II **180–81**, 303
  The big towel **179**, 303
Power Institute, University of Sydney 115, 128, 147
Pratt, Douglas 284n13
Presley, Elvis 78, 80–81
Prince, Richard 237, 256, 297
  Untitled (cowboy) **256–57**, 303
psychedelic designs 120, 141, 145, 156, 166
Public view exhibition, Potts Point (Sydney), 1970 216
publications
  art books and magazines 11, 13, 139, 143, 146–47, 150, 234, 236, 237
  Oz magazine 140–41, 166
  TV documentary 39, 42, 284n7, 293

Ramos, Mel 61
Rauschenberg, Robert 20–21, 62, 64, 76, 84, 140, 145, 152, 281n10, 297–98
  Bed 20
  Dylaby 21, **32**, **33**, 143, 303
  Quote 84, **85**, 303
Raysse, Martial 21, 112–13, 116, 298
  Rear view mirror 112–13, **116–17**, 303
readymade 20, 21, 37, 56, 62–64, 112, 116, 124, 128, 134, 237, 261, 292–93, 295, 297–98
readymades 20, 261, 278, 281n18
realism 11, 37, 139
Recent British art: a Peter Stuyvesant Foundation collection exhibition, Art Gallery of South Australia, Adelaide, 1970 285n57
Reinhard, Ken 139, 140, 146, 162, 285n69, 298
  EK 146, **208**, 303
  The public private preview 139
  Ticket box **162–63**, 303
reproductive processes 63, 84, 90, 112–13, 132, 234
Restany, Pierre 21, 112, 206, 292
Richter, Gerhard 112, 113–14, 124, 298

Helga Matura with her fiancé 114, 124, **125**, 303
Hotel Diana 114, **126**, 302

Rivers, Larry 48, 143, 145
Rooney, Robert 139, 145, 174, 234, 236, 298
  Howard Arkley (photograph) *315*
  Maria Kozic and Philip Brophy (photograph) *315*
  Superknit 1 145, **174–75**, 303
  The setting sun **264**, 303
  Tumult in the clouds **264**, 303
Rosenberg, Harold 20
Rosenquist, James 21, 62, 63, 74, 145, 188, 298, *310*
  F-111 143, 188, **200–01**, 222, 304
  Silver skies **74–75**, 304, *312*
Rosler, Martha 190–91, 298
  House beautiful: bringing the war home series 191, 196, **197–99**, 304
  Balloons **199**, 304
  Beauty rest **199**, 304
  Booby trap **197**, 304
  Boy's room **197**, 304
  Cleaning the drapes 196, **198**, 304
  Empty boys **198**, 304
  First Lady (Pat Nixon) **197**, 304
  Honors (striped burial) **199**, 304
  House beautiful, Giacometti 196, **198**, 304
  Makeup/Hands up **199**, 304
  Patio view **197**, 304
  Playboy (on view) **199**, 304
  Red stripe kitchen **197**, 304
  Roadside ambush 196, **198**, 304
  Runway **197**, 304
  Scatter **198–99**, 304
  Tract house soldier **197–98**, 304
  Tron (amputee) **198**, 304
  Vacation getaway **199**, 304
  Woman with cannon (dots) **197**, 304
Rotella, Mimmo 21
Royal College of Art, London 12, 36, 38, 42, 281n12, 284n20
Ruscha, Edward 62, 76, 190, 212, 298
  Every building on the Sunset Strip **105**, 304
  Gospel 212, **213**, 304
  Nine swimming pools and a broken glass **104**, 304
  Noise, pencil, broken pencil, cheap Western 76, **77**, 304
  Twentysix gasoline stations **104**, 304

Saint Phalle, Niki de 21, 112, 113, 120, 212, 298–99
  Black beauty 113, 120, **121**, 304
  Nana series 113, 115, 120
  She: a cathedral **110**, 120
Sale, Julia
  sculpture at The Yellow House 217
Sansom, Gareth 139, 143–44, 147, 299
  The great democracy 144, **170**, 304
Scandinavian artists 12, 114–15
'School of London' 38
Schwitters, Kurt 18, 21, 78, 281n6, 297
screenprinting 20, 37, 64, 80, 84
Scull, Robert 75; and Ethel *312*
sculpture 36, 38, 78, 106, 150, 189
'second degree' aesthetic 235, 236, 266
  see also appropriation practices
Seductive subversion: women artists and pop 1958–1968 exhibition, Philadelphia, 2010 190
sexuality 38, 54, 145, 156, 161, 189, 190, 206 *see also* eroticism
Sharp, Martin 139, 140–41, 147, 166, 190, 285n26, 299, *315*, *318*
  'artoons' 218, *318*
  Fantomas Hall, The Yellow House 217
  Jimi Hendrix **169**, 190, 304
  Legalise cannabis: the putting together of the heads **168**, 304
  Live give love **168**, 304
  Magritte Room, The Yellow House 217

Mister Tambourine Man 166, **167**, 304
  Sex **168**, 304
  Stone Room, The Yellow House 217
  Sunshine Superman 304
Sharp, Martin and Tim Lewis
  Still life 218, **219**, 304
  The unexpected answer (Yellow House) **221**, 304
Shaw, Michael Allen 139, 140, *142*, 284n20, 299
  Lawrence diptych 140, **164–65**, 304
Shead, Garry 140, 141, 144, 285n26, 299
  Bondi 144, **178**, 304
Sherman, Cindy 237, 254, 256, 299
  Untitled **254**, 304
  Untitled #92 304
  Untitled #93 304
  Untitled #113 **254**, 304
  Untitled film stills: #3, #35, #46, #50, #52 **255**, 304
Shrimpton, Jean *310*
'sinister Pop' 191
slogans 37, 42, 128, 237, 296
Smith, Bernard 115, 138, 146–47
Smithson, Peter and Alison 18
social change 12, 18, 36–39, 138, 189
  see also popular culture
Sonnabend, Ileana 124, 143, 285n39, *312*
Spoerri, Daniel 21, 295
Stedelijk Museum, Amsterdam 21, 112
Steinberg, Leo 64–65, 236
Subterranean Imitation Realists 138–39, 148 *see also* Annandale Imitation Realists (AIR)
Sulman Art Prize 1964 139
surf culture *see* beach culture
surrealism 18, 297

Tate Gallery, London 36, 161, 285n31
Taylor, Paul 13, 147, 234–35, 236, 237
techniques and materials 11, 20–21, 63–65, 75, 84, 112, 146, 230, 234–36, 281n10 *see also* Benday dots; collage and assemblage; found objects and images; reproductive processes
teen culture *see* youth culture
television documentary on pop art 39, 42, 284n7, 293
Thiebaud, Wayne 21, 299
  Delicatessen counter **73**, 304
This is tomorrow exhibition, Whitechapel Art Gallery, London, 1956 *16*, 19, 139, 140
Thomas, Daniel 138, 139, *142*, 146, 147, 161
Thomas, Laurie 139
Thoms, Albie 216, 285n26
Thomson, Gordon 115
Thornton, Wallace 140, 145, 161, 284n18
Three trends in contemporary French art touring exhibition, 1969 115
Tillers, Imants 234, 235, 236, 299
  White Aborigines **244–45**, 304
Tilson, Joe 37, 115, 143, 299, *310*
  Nine elements 37, **51**, 304
Tinguely, Jean 21
  She: a cathedral (with Saint Phalle and Ultvedt) **110**, 120
Traviato, Ralph 234
Tsk Tsk Tsk ⟶ 234, 236, 287n5(2), 296
Tuckson, Tony 152, 299–300
  Pyjamas and Herald **152–53**, 304
Twiggy (model) 240
Two decades of American painting touring exhibition,1967 115, 145, 147
Tyndall, Peter 234, 236, 300
  Title: detail: A Person Looks At A Work Of Art/ someone looks at something. LOGOS/ HA HA … **246–47**, 304
Tzara, Tristan 18

Ultvedt, Per Olof 21
  She: a cathedral (with Saint Phalle and Tinguely) **110**, 120
United Kingdom *see* British pop art; British popular culture

University of Sydney Power Institute 115, 128, 147

Vietnam War 135, 138, 188, 190, 196, 222, 298
violence 90, 113–14, 124, 188, 191, 222, 250
Voelcker, John 19
Vostell, Wolf
  Starfighter **127**, 302

Walker, Robert *142*
Walsh, Richard 140–41
war 188, 190, 196, 222, 294
Warhol, Andy 11, 13, 20, 21, 65, 80, 124, 141, 145, 188, 236, 276, 278, 300, *307*, *310*, *316*
  Bonwit Teller store display 113
  Campbell's soup 1 80, **96–97**, 305
  Electric chair **98–99**, 305
  Flowers series 143
  Heinz Tomato Ketchup boxes **95**, 305
  Jackie **83**, 305
  Mao 188–89, **203**, 305
  Marilyn Monroe 37, **100–01**, 250, 254, 305
  Mona Lisa **238–39**, 305
  Retrospective and *Reversal* series 13, 236
  Screen test: Bob Dylan **103**, 305
  Screen test: Edie Sedgwick **102**, 305
  Screen test: Lou Reed **102**, 305
  Screen test: Marcel Duchamp **103**, 305
  Self-portrait no 9 276, **277**, 305
  Silver Liz [Studio type] **82**, 305
  Triple Elvis 80, **81**, 305
Warhol, Andy and Jean-Michel Basquiat
  Collaboration **270–71**, 301
  Ten punching bags (Last Supper) **272–73**, 301
Watkins, Dick 139, 140, *142*, 144, 300
  The fall no 1 144, **172**, 305
  The fall no 2 144, **173**, 305
Watson, Jenny 234, 235–36, 240, 300
  A painted page 1: Twiggy by Richard Avedon 235, **240–41**, 305
  A painted page: pages 52 and 53 of "In the gutter" (The ears) 235, **242**, 305
  A painted page: the Herald 21/11/79 235, **243**, 305
Watters Gallery, Sydney 140, 144, 145, 146, 156, 161, 230
Wayne, John 78
Weight, Greg
  photographs, Infinity Room, The Yellow House 217
Wesselmann, Tom 21, 61, 62, 88, 141, 189, 300, *310*
  Great American nude series 88, 143, 189, 250, 300
  Smoker #11 189, **215**, 305
  Still life #29 **88–89**, 305
Westerns (movies, comic books) 76–81, 256–57
Whiteley, Brett 141, 143, 216, 222, 300, *314*
  The American Dream 143, 222, **223–26**, 305
women artists 11, 38–39, 78, 112, 113, 120, 145, 190–91, 240, 254
women, representation of 38, 113, 116, 120, 145–46, 156, 189, 190, 206, 254, 292, 295, 297, 298

The Yellow House, Potts Point (Sydney) 147, 216, *217*, 218, *318*
Young British painters exhibition, Art Gallery of NSW, Sydney, 1964 143
Young contemporaries exhibitions
  London,1959 284n20
  London,1960s 12, 19, 36, 37, 38, 140, 292, 293, 294, 295, 297
  Sydney, 1964 and 1965 139, 299
youth culture 37–38, 40, 42, 138, 140, 190
  see also popular culture

films and film stars 60, 61, 78, 80, 90, 140, 161, 300
  Elvis Presley 78, 80, *81*
  Marilyn Monroe 19, 37, 39, *100–01*, 218, *219*, 250, 254
  Westerns 76–81, 256–57
fine art tradition 36, 38
  and mass culture 60, 112
Fischer, Konrad 114
flags in art 20–21, 37, 42, 64
Fletcher, Paul 234, 236
found objects and images 11, 12, 18, 20, 21, 36, 54, 78, 88, 114, 138–39, 148, 218, 222 *see also* readymade/s, collage and assemblage
French art/artists 12, 18, 20, 21, 112–13, 115, 120

Gainsbourg, Serge *313*
gender roles 36, 38, 62, 206, 296, 298, 299
Germany 12, 112, 113–14, 124
Giacometti, Alberto 18, 297
Gilbert & George 237, 294
  Friendship **274–75**, 302
Ginger Meggs Memorial School of Art, Sydney 216
Gittoes, George
  Puppet Theatre, The Yellow House 216, *217*
  Stone Room, The Yellow House *217*
Gittoes, Joyce
  Stone Room, The Yellow House 216, *217*
Glasheen, Michael 141
Gleeson, James 139, 146–47, 161, 284n18
Grafik des Kapitalistischen Realismus (Graphics of Capitalist Realism) print portfolio 114, *126*, 302
The great nostalgia show, Central Street Gallery, Sydney, 1969 144
Greenberg, Clement 20

Hamilton, Richard 11, 18, 19–20, 36, 192, 294
  Adonis in Y fronts 37, **53**, 302
  Carapace **27**, 302
  Fashion-plate 302
  Just what is it that makes today's homes so different, so appealing? (1956) 19, 36, 188
  Just what was it that made yesterday's homes so different, so appealing? Upgrade **29**, 281n14, 302
  Kent State 188, **194**, 302
  My Marilyn **8**, 37, **53**, 302
  Swingeing London '67 – etching **193**, 302
  Swingeing London 67 – sketch 192, **193**, 302
  Toaster 302
Hamilton, Terry 19
Hanson, Duane 191, 294
  Woman with a laundry basket 191, **214**, 302
hard-edge style 143, 144, 145, 147
Haring, Keith 232, 237, 294, *317*
  Untitled **268–69**, 302
Henderson, Nigel 18
Hess, Thomas 39
Hirst, Damien 261
Hockney, David 34, 36, 37, 38, 39, 54, 143, 190, 210, 294, *308*, *310*
  I saw in Louisana a live-oak growing 143
  Man in shower in Beverly Hills 54, **55**, 302
  Portrait of an artist **210–11**, 302
  The second marriage 38, **46–47**, 143, 302, *308*
  Two friends 143
  We two boys together clinging 38, **44**, 302
Hödicke, KH
  Magic window cleaner II **126**, 302
Hollywood *see* films and film stars
homosexuality 38, 54
Hughes, Robert 141, 147, 150, 188
humour 128, 174
Hutchison, Max 140
Hutchison, Noel 144

'Imitation Realism' 138 *see also* Annandale Imitation Realists (AIR)
Independent Group, Institute of Contemporary Arts, London 18–19, 36, 37, 139, 281n3(1), 281n12, 297
Indiana, Robert 21, 61, 62, 92, 295, *312*
  Love cross **109**, 302, *312*
  The Demuth American dream no 5 62, 92, **93**, 302
Institute of Contemporary Arts, London 18, 38
Institute of Modern Art, Brisbane 240
international pop art exhibitions in Australia 11, 143, 144, 145, 237, 285n46, 285n57
Italian art/artists 12, 114–15

Jacquet, Alain 112, 295, *313*
  Déjeuner sur l'herbe (diptych) **14–15**, 112, **119**, 302
  Portrait d'homme (Portrait of a man) 112, **118**, 302
Janis, Sidney 21
Johns, Jasper 20–21, 63, 76, 143, 145, 212, 295
  Flag 20–21
  White numbers 21, **31**, 302
Jones, Allen 36, 37, 38, 48, 115, 189, 295, *310*, *313*
  Come in 147, 189, **204**, 302
  Hatstand, Table and Chair 38
  Reflected man 38, 48, **49**, 302
  Secretary 189, **205**, 302
junk materials *see* found objects and images

Kaldor, John 143
Kapitalistischen Realismus (Capitalist Realism) 113, 114, 126, 296, 297, 298
Kapitalistischen Realisten (Capitalist Realists) 112, 113, 115, 298
Kennedy, Jackie 83
Kennedy, John F 84, 222
Kerouac, Jack 148
Kienholz, Edward 191, 295
  Sawdy 191, **195**, 302
King, Martin Luther 188, 222
Kingston, Peter 141, 295
  Stone Room, The Yellow House 216, *217*
  The checkout chicks **220**, 302
Kitaj, RB 36, 37, 38, 56, 140, 284n19, 295
  Walter Lippmann 56, **57**, 302
Kitchen Sink School 140, 147
kitsch 20, 80, 154, 292
Klein, Yves 21, 112
Koons, Jeff 189, 237, 261, 295
  New Hoover Convertibles **260**, 302
  Three ball 50/50 tank (Spalding Dr JK Silver series) **261**, 302
  Vase of flowers **263**, 302
Kozic, Maria 234, 236, 278, 295–96, *315*
  MASTERPIECES (Warhol) 278, **279**, 302
Kruger, Barbara 191, 237, 256, 296
  Untitled (you can't drag your money into the grave with you) **258–59**, 302
Kuttner, Manfred 112, 113

Laing, Gerald *310*
Lanceley, Colin *136*, 138, 139, 141, 150, 296
  Love me stripper 150, **151**, 302
Lanceley, Colin, Mike Brown and Ross Crothall
  Byzantium **136**, 148, **149**, 301
Larter, Richard 139, 140, 147, 161, 189, 230, 296
  Big time easy mix 189, **228–29**, 303
  collages:
    Being dead **160**, 302
    Quick whirl round the puppet gallery **160**, 302
    The deadheart of illusions **160**, 302
    Untitled [figures and bomb] **160**, 302
    Untitled [figures and factory] **160**, 302
    Untitled [figures and shark] **160**, 302

Dithyrambic painting no 6 **161**, 302
Prompt Careb and how we never learn 189–90, 230, **231**, 303
The hairdresser **177**, 303
Ledeboer, Peter 166
Leo Castelli Gallery, New York 21, 144, 285n39, 295, 296
Lewinski, Jorge
  Peter Blake (photograph) *311*
Lewis, Tim 218, 296
Lewis, Tim and Martin Sharp 141, 296
  Still life 218, **219**, 304
  The unexpected answer (Yellow House) **221**, 304
Lichtenstein, Roy 19, 21, *58*, 63, 64, 68, 124, 141, 145, 190, 236, 278, 296, *310*
  Bull I–VI **202**, 303
  In the car **86–87**, 303
  Kitchen range **70**, 303, *312*
  Look Mickey *58*, **68–69**, 236, 303
  Peanut butter cup 143, 303
  Woman in bath **71**, 303
Lippard, Lucy 61, 128, 145, 285n40, 300
Lippmann, Walter 56
London 12, 18–19, 36, 39, 140, 141, 166, 190, 192 *see also* British pop art; British popular culture
Los Angeles 54, 76, 80, 116, 212, 278, 294, 295, 298
Lueg, Konrad 112, 113, 114, 296
  Babies **127**, 302
  Football players **123**, 303
Lynn, Elwyn 139, 140, 143, 150

McCaughey, Patrick 145
Macdonald, Dwight 60, 61
McGrath, Sandra 161
McGregor, Craig 141
McHale, John 18, 19
McLean, Bridgid 146, 296
  Stop **185**, 303
  Untitled **4**, **184**, 303
McLuhan, Marshall 37, 60, 64, 138, 281n9
magazines/art publications 13, 139, 143, 150, 234, 236, 237
  Oz magazine 140–41, 166
Marisol 21, 78, 296–97, *309*
  John Wayne **78–79**, 303
mass culture *see* popular culture
mass media 11, 12–13, 21, 39, 60, 132, 138
mass media imagery 18–20, 39, 48, 60, 62–63, 132, 138–39, 146, 161; death and misfortune 113–14, 124
materials *see* techniques and materials
mechanical reproduction *see* reproductive processes
media (mass media) *see* mass media
Milan 114, 115
Milgate, Rodney 156
Modern art in the United States: a selection from the collections of the Museum of Modern Art, New York exhibition, Tate Gallery, London, 1956 36
modernism 12–13, 61–62
Monroe, Marilyn: imagery 19, 37, 39, *100–01*, 218, *219*, 250, 254
Morland, Francis *310*
Morley, Lewis
  Pauline Boty (photograph) *311*
mortality *see* death and misfortune
movies *see* films and film stars
Museum of Modern Art, New York 21, 36, 60, 78, 138, 145, 237
Museum of Modern Art of Australia, Melbourne 138, 148
music 62, 138, 190, 234, 236

National Gallery of Victoria, Melbourne 115, 143
neo-dada 11, 21, 78, 112
Neville, Richard 141, 166, 285n26
'new American dreamers' 62
The new American painting exhibition, Tate Gallery, London, 1959 36

The new generation exhibition, Whitechapel Art Gallery, London, 1964 54
New painting of common objects exhibition, Pasadena Art Museum, 1962 76, 298
new realism 11, 21, 62
New realists exhibition, Sidney Janis Gallery, New York, 1962 21, 74, 88, 294, 298, 299, 300
new social realism 62
'new wave' subculture 234–35
New York 20, 39, 62, 112, 114, 140, 143
New York School painters 36, 62, 68
Nixon, John 234
Nolan, Sidney 138, 282n10
Noland, Kenneth 37, 140
Le nouveaux réalisme à Paris et à New York exhibition, Galerie Rive Droite, Paris, 1961 21
nouveaux réalisme (new realism) group 21, 112–13, 115, 120
nudes 189, 190, 206
  see also eroticism; sexuality

obscenity prosecutions 140–41, 154
October journal 236, 237
Oh what a beaut view and other paintings exhibition, Sydney, 1968 144
Oldenburg, Claes 11, 21, 106, 141, 297, *310*, *311*
  Giant 3-way plug scale B **106**, 303
  Giant soft fan – ghost version 106, **107**, 303, *311*
  Leopard chair **94**, 303
  Soft hot and cold taps 143
Oldfield, Alan 144–45, 297
  Cliché 144, **171**, 303
Olsen, John 138, 294, 297
Oz magazine 140–41, 166
Oz supa art market exhibition, Clune Galleries, Potts Point (Sydney), 1966 141, 295

Paintin' a-go-go exhibition, Gallery A, Paddington (Sydney), 1965 140, 154
painting 36–38, 54, 56, 62, 84, 234
Paolozzi, Eduardo 18–19, 36, 140, 230, 285n25, 297
  Bunk collages 18–19
  Bunk! Evadne in green dimension 19, **26**, 303
  Hazards include dust, hailstones and bullets; Survival **25**, 303
  Headlines from horrors ville **24**, 303
  I was a rich man's plaything **22**, 188, 303
  It's a psychological fact pleasure helps your disposition **23**, 303
  Lessons of last time **24**, 303
  Man holds the key **23**, 303
  Markoni capital 36, **50**, 303
  Meet the people **23**, 303
  Merry Xmas with T-1 space suits **25**, 303
  No one's sure how good it is **25**, 303
  Real gold **25**, 303
  Sack-o-sauce **25**, 303
  The ultimate planet **24**, 303
  Was this metal monster master – or slave? **23**, 303
  Will man outgrow the Earth **25**, 303
  Windtunnel test **24**, 303
  You can't beat the real thing **25**, 303
  You'll soon be congratulating yourself **25**, 303
  Yours till the boys come home **25**, 303
Paris 18, 20, 120
  see also French art/artists
Paris Biennale of Young Artists, Musée d'Art Moderne de la Ville de Paris, 1963 *310*
Phillips, Peter 36, 37–38, 297, *310*
  Motorpsycho / Tiger 38, **45**, 303
photography and photographic images 37, 63, 64, 124, 190–91, 192, 196, 210, 234, 254, 256, 274 *see also* found objects and images; mass media imagery
'Pictures Generation' 236–37, 256

Page numbers in *italic* indicate illustrations.
Page numbers in the form 282n10 indicate
page and note number; the column is
added in parentheses where needed for
identification: 282n10(1)

abstract expressionism 20, 36–37, 48,
   61–62, 145
abstraction 36, 37, 39, 48, 138, 144, 145,
   147, 152
Adami, Valerio 112, 115, 250, 292
   F Lensky all'International Dance Studio
      (F Lensky at the International Dance
      Studio) 115, *131*, 301
advertising art *see* commercial art
Allen, John 141
Alloway, Lawrence 18, 36, 39, 281n5(3)
American pop art 12, 60–109
   achievements 64–65
   at *Documenta IV* exhibition 115
   content and visual language 60–63, 88
   criticisms of 60–61, 112
   emergence 60
   popularity 60, 61
   techniques and materials 61, 62, 63–65,
      75, 84, 281n10
   works *67–109*
American popular culture 12, 19, 20, 21,
   36–37, 60–62
   pervasiveness 42, 138, 143
American prints and posters exhibition,
   Central Street Gallery, Sydney, 1967
   285n46
The American supermarket exhibition,
   Bianchini Gallery, New York, 1964 141
America's west *see* Westerns (movies,
   comic books)
'angry young men' 36
Annandale Imitation Realists (AIR) 138–39,
   141, 145, 147, 148, 150, 284n3(3)
   Byzantium *136*, 148, *149*
Annear, Judy 234
the Antipodeans 138, 147
Apple, Billy 37, 141
appropriation practices 13, 234–36, 240,
   250, 256, 261, 266, 276, 278
Arkley, Howard 234, 237, 266, 292, *315*
   Family home: suburban exterior 266
   Primitive gold **265**, 301
   Triple fronted **266–67**, 301
Art & Text magazine 13, 234, 237
Art and Australia magazine 139
art books and magazines 11, 12, 139,
   143, 146–47, 150, 234, 236, 237
Art for Mart's sake exhibition, Clune
   Galleries, Potts Point (Sydney), 1965 141
Art Gallery of New South Wales 139, 161
Art in the age of mechanical reproduction
   exhibition, George Paton Gallery,
   Melbourne, 1982 234
The art of assemblage exhibition, Museum of
   Modern Art, New York, 1961 21, 78, 138
Arty Wild Oat (newspaper) 140, 141, 299
Aspects of new British art exhibition, Art
   Gallery of New South Wales, Sydney
   1967 48, 285n57
assassinations 39, 84, 188, 222
assemblage *see* collage and assemblage
Atlas, Charles 19
Australian art 138, 147, 234–35
   convergence of art and music 234
   market 154
   pop *see* Australian pop art
Australian expatriate artists 12, 39, 140,
   141, 143, 166, 190, 282n10(1), 282n12(1)
Australian painting today: a survey of the
   past ten years touring exhibition, 1963–64
   139, 154
Australian pop art 12, 138–85
   collage and assemblage 138–39, 145,
      148, 152, 222, 284n12
   content and visual language 139–40,
      147
   development 12, 138
   influences on 11, 12, 115, 138–39, 140,
      143, 144, 147

responses to 139–41, 144, 146–47,
   154, 156
works *148–85*
Axell, Evelyne *186*, 190, 206, 292
   La grande sortie dans l'Espace *186*
   Le retour de Tarzan 190, 206, **207**, 301

Bacon, Francis 38, 54, 141, 143, 144,
   146, 147, 295, 299
Baj, Enrico 21, 114–15, 128, 292, *313*
   General *128*, 301
   Le Baron Robert Olive de Plassey,
      Gouverneur de Bengale (The Baron
      Robert Olive de Plassey, Governor
      of Bengal) 114–15, *129*, 301
Banham, Reyner 18
Basquiat, Jean-Michel 237, 292, *316*
Basquiat, Jean-Michel and Andy Warhol
   Collaboration **270–71**, 301
   Ten punching bags (Last Supper)
      272–73, 301
Bates, Barrie 37
beach culture 146, 180, 283n4(4)
The Beatles 37, 138, 140
Benday dots 64, 68, 114, 230, 278,
   295, 296
Berges furniture store, Düsseldorf 113
Binns, Vivienne 145, 156, 292
   Phallic monument 145, *158*, 301
   Suggon 145, *159*, 301
   Vag dens 145, 156, *157*, 301
Blake, Peter 36, 37, 40, 292–93, 299,
   310, *311*
   Self-portrait with badges 37, 40, *41*, 301
   The first real target 37, 40, **40**, 301
Bonwit Teller department store,
   New York 113
books *see* art books and magazines
Boshier, Derek *34*, 36, 37, 42, 293, *310*
   Drinka pinta milka 37, 42, *43*, 301
Boty, Pauline 36, 37, 38–39, 206, *311*
Boynes, Robert 11, 146, 293
   Playboy club news *183*, 301
   Premonition 146, *182*, 301
Brack, John 138, 284n2(3)
Brehmer, KP
   The sensuality between fingertips
      127, 302
British pop art 12, 36–57
   emergence 18–20, 139
   end 39
   impact on Australian artists 140, 143,
      147, 282n10(1)
   works *40–57*
British popular culture 12, 18–20, 37, 39,
   114, 143
Brophy, Philip 234, 235, *315*
Brown, Mike 11, *136*, 138, 139, 140,
   145, 147, 148, 154, 285n58, 293
   Arbitrary trisection with figtrees and later
      enthusiastic additions *155*, 301
   Big mess *176*, 301
   Hallelujah! *154*, 301
   Mary Lou / Mary Lou as Miss Universe
      139, 154
   Tom 301
Brown, Mike and Ross Crothall
   Sailing to Byzantium *148*, 301
Brown, Mike, Ross Crothall and
   Colin Lanceley
   Byzantium *136*, 148, *149*, 301
Butler, Rex 234

Cage, John 20, 63–64
capitalism 12, 113, 222, 292
Capitalist Realism *see* Kapitalistischen
   Realismus
Capitalist Realists *see* Kapitalistischen
   Realisten
Caulfield, Patrick 36, 190, 293
   Dining recess *209*, 301
celebrities *see* films and film stars
censorship 140–41, 154, 190
Central Street Gallery, Sydney 144
Central Street style 144

Chesworth, David 234, 236
cinema *see* films and film stars
Clune Galleries, Potts Point (Sydney) 141,
   143 *see also* Yellow House
Cold War 132, 138, 222
collage and assemblage 12, 18–21, 36–37,
   88, 90, 128, 132, 138–40, 145, 148,
   150, 152, 222, 284n12 *see also* found
   objects and images
Collages and objects exhibition, Institute
   of Contemporary Arts, London, 1954 19
colour field style 64, 144, 145
'combines' *see* collage and assemblage
commercial art 11, 19–20, 36, 68, 76, 88,
   112, 146, 188, 256
'common object painting' 62, 112
'commonism' 62
consumerism 11, 12, 13, 18, 20, 42,
   60–61, 62–63, 65, 90, 106, 138, 191, 196
Contemporary American painting, selected
   from the James A Michener Foundation
   collection touring exhibition, 1964 143
Contemporary Art Society 143, 284n17
Cordell, Magda 19
cowboys *see* Westerns (movies, comics)
Cox, Ian 234, 236
Crothall, Ross 138, 139, 148, 293
Crothall, Ross and Mike Brown
   Sailing to Byzantium *148*, 301
Crothall, Ross, Mike Brown
   and Colin Lanceley
   Byzantium *136*, 148, *149*, 301

dada movement 11, 21 *see also* neo-dada
Danto, Arthur 65
Davie, Ben 141
Davila, Juan 234, 235–36, 250, 293
   Miss Sigmund 250, **251**, 301
   Neo-pop **252–53**, 301
de Kooning, Willem 37, 150, 297, 299, 300
death and misfortune 113–14, 124, 143,
   188–89
department stores: displays and
   performances 113
Dine, Jim 21, 143, 293
   An animal **67**, 301
Documenta exhibitions, Kassel, West
   Germany 12, 115, 143, 292, 293, 298
Drexler, Rosalyn 61, 90, 293–94
   Home movies **90–91**, 301
   Race for time **91**, 301
Dubuffet, Jean 18, 38, 143, 296, 297
Duchamp, Marcel 18, 20, 21, *103*, 281n18
Dunn, Richard 234, 236, 294
   Relief picture and figure 10 **248–49**, 301
Düsseldorf Academy 113, 114
Dylaby: Dynamisch labyrint, Stedelijk
   Museum, Amsterdam, 1962 21
Dylan, Bob *103*, 166

England *see* British pop art;
   British popular culture
Ernst, Max 18
eroticism 38, 144, 145, 156, 189, 206,
   250, 292, 295, 298, 300
Erró 114, 132, 294
   Pop's history 114, **132–33**, 301
European pop art 12, 112–35
   politically engaged art 114
   reception in Australia 115
   works *116–35*
exhibitions of international pop art works
   in Australia 11, 143, 144, 145, 237,
   285n46, 285n57
expatriates *see* Australian expatriate artists

The Factory 61, 188, 300, *310*
factualism 11
Fahlström, Öyvind 112, 114, 134–35, 294
   ESSO-LSD 114, **134–35**, 302
fashion *see* popular culture
The field exhibition, National Gallery of
   Victoria, Melbourne, 1968 144, 145
figurative art 11, 39, 48, 138, 144, 147

Acknowledgments

I would like to thank Michael Brand, who programmed *Pop to popism* soon after becoming the director of the Art Gallery of New South Wales, for his commitment throughout several years of research, development and loan negotiations. Anne Flanagan, deputy director, and Suhanya Raffel, director of collections, both provided unstinting support. Charlotte Davy, senior manager of exhibitions, has been instrumental in delivering this exhibition.

Anneke Jaspers, assistant curator of contemporary art, has worked on this exhibition from the outset and it could not have been realised without her commitment and exemplary work, particularly managing the program of original research on pop art in Australia, and in her role as co-editor and writer for this book. I also acknowledge Jade Williamson and Faith Chisholm for their meticulous research and invaluable curatorial support.

The realisation of an exhibition and its supporting productions and programs is only possible through the dedicated and talented staff at the Gallery. In particular I would like to acknowledge Tanguy Le Moing for the exhibition design, assisted by Caitlin Seymour-King; Julie Donaldson's management of and Analiese Cairis's exceptional design for this publication, and Cara Hickman's calmness with a tight production schedule; the indispensable assistance of librarians Eric Riddler, Claire Eggleston and Vivian Huang; Nick Yelverton for cataloguing; Rachel Scott, Gitte Weise, and interns Sushma Griffin and Christiane Keys-Statham for additional research; Charlotte Cox for exhibition registration; Megan Young's coordination of image rights; the contribution of the conservation team; Jacquie Riddell and Sangeeta Chandra on the marketing campaign; Robert Herbert for the film program; Sheona White, Josephine Touma, Alexandra Gregg, Victoria Collings and Leeanne Carr for the programs and education initiatives; and Francesca Ford and Penny Sanderson for leading the digital interpretation project. For securing funding I thank Kirsty Divehall, Arabella Rayner and Penny Cooper; and for the range of merchandise I thank Rebecca Allport, Maryanne Marsh, Zinnia O'Brien and the team in the Gallery Shop. And special thanks to Claire Martin for her work on the media campaign.

I am also grateful to the many people who work to transform our galleries into an exhibition experience. I thank Luke Simkins and his team of builders; Michael Brown and the painting team; Nik Reith and the installation team; Simm Steel for lighting; and Mark Taylor for audiovisual. I also thank my curatorial colleagues – senior curators Deborah Edwards and Judy Annear – and my colleagues in the prints study room, photography, philanthropy, events, security, visitor services, ticketing and information desk, our volunteer guides; and Judith White and Jill Sykes in the AGNSW Society.

My thanks go to the commissioned writers of the essays for the book: Michael Desmond, Chris McAuliffe, Justin Paton and Ann Stephen; to the Gallery entry writers; to Jaime Tsai for her work on the artist biographies; and to text editor Paige Amor. I would also like to particularly thank Mark Hughes for his generous supply of contacts and introductions, particularly into private collections in America, from which major loans were secured for this exhibition. I also extend my gratitude to Mark Ledbury, director, Power Institute, University of Sydney, for partnering with the Art Gallery of New South Wales on programs.

This exhibition would not have been possible without the generosity and information sharing of our many colleagues and lenders, for which I am very grateful. I thank the following:

Australia and NZ: I warmly thank the National Gallery of Australia, Canberra, which is the biggest single lender to the exhibition: director Ron Radford, who generously approved our extensive loan request, supported by senior curators Christine Dixon, international painting and sculpture; Jane Kinsman, international prints, drawings and illustrated books; Deborah Hart, Australian paintings and sculpture post 1920; and Roger Butler, Australian prints and drawings. I would also like to thank curator Jaklyn Babington, assistant curator Lara Nicholls and collection study room coordinator Rose Montebello. And in addition I thank: Nick Mitzevich, director, and Jane Messenger, curator of European and North American art, Art Gallery of South Australia, Adelaide; Stefano Carboni, director, Jenepher Duncan, curator of contemporary Australian art, and Gary Dufour, then deputy director and chief curator, Art Gallery of Western Australia; Elizabeth Ann Macgregor, director, Glenn Barkley, (previously) senior curator, and Natasha Bullock, senior curator, Museum of Contemporary Art Australia; Tony Ellwood, director, Kirsty Grant, head of Australian art, and Beckett Rozentals, assistant curator, National Gallery of Victoria, Melbourne; Chris Saines, director, and curatorial managers Julie Ewington, Australian art, and Kathryn Weir, international art and Australian cinémathèque, Queensland Art Gallery | Gallery of Modern Art, Brisbane; David Ellis, director, and Ann Stephen, senior curator, University Art Gallery and Art Collections, University of Sydney; Campbell Gray, director, The University of Queensland Art Museum; Rhana Devenport, director, Auckland Art Gallery Toi o Tāmaki; Charles Nodrum; Helen Eager and Christopher Hodges; Noel Hutchison; John Kaldor; Kerry Stokes, Sarah Yukich and Erica Persak, Kerry Stokes Collection, Perth; Jenny Watson and Anna Schwartz.

UK: Caroline Douglas, head of Arts Council Collection, and Jill Constantine, senior curator, Arts Council Collection, Southbank Centre, London; Jessica Corbet-McBride, Halcyon Gallery, London; Kate Davies, Murderme Collection; Sir John Leighton, director-general, National Galleries of Scotland; Simon Groom, director, and Patrick Elliott, senior curator, Scottish National Gallery of Modern Art; Paul Thompson, rector, the custodians of the collection, and Neil Parkinson, archives and collections manager, Royal College of Art, London; Sir Nicholas Serota, director Tate, Caroline Collier, director Tate National, and Jessica Morgan, Daskalopoulos curator, international art, Tate Modern; Martin Roth, director, and Catherine Flood, curator, prints, word and image department, Victoria and Albert Museum.

USA: Janne Sirén, Peggy Pierce Elfin director, and Holly E Hughes, curator for the collection, Albright-Knox Art Gallery, Buffalo, New York; Eric C Shiner, director, Nicholas Chambers, The Milton Fine curator of art and Geralyn Huxley, curator of film and video, The Andy Warhol Museum, Pittsburgh; Matthew Teitelbaum, Michael and Sonja Koerner director and CEO, and Kitty Scott, curator of modern and contemporary art, Art Gallery of Ontario, Toronto; William Hennessey, director, Chrysler Museum of Art, Norfolk; Blake Milteer, museum director and chief curator, and Michael Howell, collections manager, Colorado Springs Fine Art Center; Richard Koshalek, (previously) director, Melissa Chiu, director, Kerry Brougher, chief curator, and Evelyn Hankins, associate curator, Hirshhorn Museum and Sculpture Garden, Smithsonian Institution, Washington, DC; Joe Lewis and Vivienne Lewis, The Lewis Collection; Josef Helfenstein, director, and Michelle White, curator, The Menil Collection, Houston; Tom Heman and Gina Guddemi, Metro Pictures, New York; Thomas P Campbell, director, and Marla Prather, curator of modern and contemporary art, The Metropolitan Museum of Art, New York; Josephine Nash, Mitchell-Innes & Nash, New York; Gary Tinterow, director, and Alison de Lima Greene, curator contemporary art and special projects, The Museum of Fine Arts, Houston; Glenn Lowry, director, Ann Tempkin, chief curator of painting and drawing, and Cora Rosevear, associate curator, The Museum of Modern Art, New York; Earl A Powell III, director, and Harry Cooper, curator and head of modern art, National Gallery of Art, Washington, DC; Christy MacLear, executive director, Robert Rauschenberg Foundation; Richard D Segal and Monica Mayer Segal, collectors, and Molly Segal, art registrar, The Seavest Collection; Alex Nyerges, director, and John B Ravenal, Sydney and Frances Lewis Family curator of modern and contemporary art, Virginia Museum of Fine Arts, Richmond; Billie Milam Weisman, director, and Mary-Ellen Powell, curatorial coordinator, Frederick R Weisman Art Foundation, Los Angeles; Claire Wesselmann and Jeffrey Sturges, Tom Wesselmann Estate. And in addition: Jay Dandy, research assistant, department of contemporary art, The Art Institute of Chicago; Sharon Avery-Fahlström; Joanne Heyler, director/chief curator, and Vicki Gambell, director of collections management, The Broad Art Foundation, Los Angeles; Colin B Bailey, director and Richard Benefield, deputy director, Fine Arts Museums of San Francisco; Susan Davidson, senior curator, collections and exhibitions, Guggenheim Museum; Stephanie Barron, chief curator of modern and contemporary art, Los Angeles County Museum of Art; Lauren Wittels, Luhring Augustine; Naomi Beckwith, Marilyn and Larry Fields curator, Museum of Contemporary Art, Chicago; Timothy Rub, George D Widener director and CEO, Philadelphia Museum of Art, Philadelphia.

Europe: Anette Kruszynski, head of the curatorial department, Kunstsammlung Nordrhein-Westfalen, Düsseldorf; José Ignacio Wert Ortega, chairman, and Guillermo Solana, artistic director, Museo Thyssen-Bornemisza, Madrid; Hafthor Yngvason, director, and Bryndís Erla Hjálmarsdóttir, project manager, Reykjavík Art Museum; Max Hollein, director, Martin Engler, curator, and Franziska Leuthäusser, curatorial assistant, contemporary art, Städel Museum, Frankfurt am Main; Beat Wismer, general director, and Kay Heymer, head of modern art, Stiftung Museum Kunstpalast, Düsseldorf; Consuelo Císcar Casabán, executive director, IVAM Valencian Institute of Modern Art, Generalitat. And in addition: Britta Schmitz, chief curator, Hamburger Bahnhof, Berlin; James S Snyder, Anne and Jerome Fisher director, Israel Museum, Jerusalem; Christoph Becker, director, Kunsthaus Zurich; Cécile Debray, curator collections modernes, Musée national d'Art Moderne/Centre Pompidou; Daniel Birnbaum, director, Moderna Museet, Stockholm; Jaroslaw Suchan, director, Museum Sztuki w Łodzi, Łodź; Dieter Scholz, curator, Neue Nationalgalerie, Berlin.

Wayne Tunnicliffe
Head curator, Australian art
and *Pop to popism* curator

Lenders

Public collections

Albright-Knox Art Gallery, Buffalo, New York
The Andy Warhol Museum, Pittsburgh
Art Gallery of Ontario, Toronto
Art Gallery of South Australia, Adelaide
Arts Council Collection, Southbank Centre, London
Chrysler Museum of Art, Norfolk
Colorado Springs Fine Art Center
Deutsche Bank Collection at the Städel Museum, Städel Museum, Frankfurt am Main
Hirshhorn Museum and Sculpture Garden, Smithsonian Institution, Washington, DC
IVAM Valencian Institute of Modern Art, Generalitat
JW Power Collection, University of Sydney, managed by Museum of Contemporary Art Australia, Sydney
Kunstsammlung Nordrhein-Westfalen, Düsseldorf
The Menil Collection, Houston
The Metropolitan Museum of Art, New York
Museo Thyssen-Bornemisza, Madrid
Museum of Contemporary Art Australia, Sydney
The Museum of Fine Arts, Houston
The Museum of Modern Art, New York
National Gallery of Art, Washington, DC
National Gallery of Australia, Canberra
National Gallery of Victoria, Melbourne
Queensland Art Gallery | Gallery of Modern Art, Brisbane
Reykjavík Art Museum
Royal College of Art, London
Scottish National Gallery of Modern Art, Edinburgh
State Art Collection, Art Gallery of Western Australia, Perth
Stiftung Museum Kunstpalast, Düsseldorf
Tate
The University of Queensland, Brisbane
Victoria and Albert Museum, London
Virginia Museum of Fine Arts, Richmond

Private galleries, collectors and artists

Charles Nodrum Gallery
Helen Eager and Christopher Hodges
The Eyles Family Collection
Frederick R Weisman Art Foundation, Los Angeles
Noel Hutchison
John Kaldor Family Collection at the Art Gallery of New South Wales
Kerry Stokes Collection, Perth
The Lewis Collection
Murderme Collection
Robert Rauschenberg Foundation
Martha Rosler and Mitchell-Innes & Nash, New York
The Seavest Collection
Cindy Sherman and Metro Pictures, New York
Jenny Watson and Anna Schwartz Gallery
Claire Wesselmann
And seven private lenders who wish to remain anonymous

Contributors

Michael Desmond is an independent curator and writer with a long history in museums and galleries including manager of the Drill Hall Gallery, Canberra; senior curator of international paintings and sculpture, National Gallery of Australia; manager of collections and research at the Powerhouse Museum; and deputy director, National Portrait Gallery, Canberra. His recent exhibitions include *Present tense: an imagined grammar of portraiture in the digital age*, National Portrait Gallery (2010) and *Trigger happy: new work by Ben Quilty*, Drill Hall Gallery (2013).

Anneke Jaspers is assistant curator, contemporary art at the Art Gallery of New South Wales and assistant curator of *Pop to popism*. Her exhibitions include *Taking form: Agatha Gothe-Snape, Sriwhana Spong*, Art Gallery of New South Wales (2013) and *Imprint*, Artspace, Sydney (2009); she was managing curator of the AGNSW Contemporary Projects series 2010–12. Her writing on contemporary art has been published nationally and internationally, most recently in the Australian Centre for Contemporary Art's exhibition catalogue *Framed movements* (2014). She was a contributing editor for the contemporary art journal *Runway* 2008–11.

Dr Chris McAuliffe is an independent scholar and curator with degrees in art history from the University of Melbourne and Harvard University. From 2000–13 he was director of the Ian Potter Museum of Art, University of Melbourne. In 2011–12, he was visiting professor of Australian Studies at Harvard University. He was the consultant curator for and author of an essay for the *America: painting a nation* exhibition and catalogue (2013). His publications include *Art and suburbia* (1996), *Linda Marrinon: let her try* (2007) and *Jon Cattapan: possible histories* (2008).

Justin Paton is head curator of international art at the Art Gallery of New South Wales. Formerly senior curator at Christchurch Art Gallery in New Zealand, he is an award-winning writer on art. His *How to look at a painting* (2005) won a Montana New Zealand Book Award, he was the recipient of the 2012 Katherine Mansfield Menton Fellowship for writers, and his co-authored *Ron Mueck* exhibition catalogue for Édition Fondation Cartier pour l'art contemporain, Paris (2013) was joint winner of the Prix CatalPa 2013. In 2013 he curated New Zealand's presentation at the Venice Biennale, *Bill Culbert: Front door out back*.

Dr Ann Stephen is senior curator at the University Art Gallery & University Art Collection, The University of Sydney. She has worked for three decades as a curator and art writer within state museums and as a freelance curator. Stephen has written widely on the visual arts, and edited and coordinated many exhibition catalogues and essays on contemporary and Indigenous art. Her books include: *On looking at looking: the art and politics of Ian Burn* (2006); *Modernism & Australia: documents on art, design and architecture 1917–1967* (2006), and *Modern times: the untold story of modernism in Australia* (2008), both co-edited with Andrew McNamara and Philip Goad.

Wayne Tunnicliffe is head curator of Australian art at the Art Gallery of New South Wales and curator of *Pop to popism*. His previous exhibitions and publications for the Gallery include the complete rehang of the Australian collection in 2012 with Deborah Edwards; *The John Kaldor Family Collection* (2011, editor); *Wilderness: contemporary Australian painting* (2010); *Tim Johnson: Painting ideas* (a 40-year survey co-curated with Julie Ewington, 2009); *Adam Cullen: Let's get lost* (2008); *Contemporary: AGNSW contemporary collection* (2006, editor); *Robert Owen: Different lights cast different shadows* (2004); and *Simryn Gill: Self selection* (2002).

Entries by Art Gallery of New South Wales staff

Faith Chisholm (FC)
researcher

Anne Gerard-Austin (AGA)
assistant curator, European art

Alexandra Gregg (AG)
coordinator, contemporary programs

Anneke Jaspers (AJ)
assistant curator, contemporary art

Steven Miller (SM)
head, research library and archive

Denise Mimmocchi (DM)
curator, Australian art

Justin Paton (JP)
head curator, international art

Anne Ryan (AR)
curator, Australian prints, drawings and watercolours

Dr Josephine Touma (JT)
senior coordinator, public programs

Wayne Tunnicliffe (WT)
head curator, Australian art

Eleanor Weber (EW)
assistant curator, photographs
(to June 2014)

Jade Williamson (JW)
assistant curator, Australian art

Natalie Wilson (NW)
curator, Australian art

Nick Yelverton (NY)
curatorial assistant, Australian art

Dr Andrew Yip (AY)
coordinator, public programs

Bibliography
compiled by
Jade Williamson

Artist biographies
Jaime Tsai
art historian and independent curator
with AGNSW curators